WELCOME TO THE WORLD OF
Kangaroos

Diane Swanson

WALRUS
B O O K S

Copyright © 2004 by Diane Swanson
Walrus Books
An imprint of Whitecap Books

Edited by Elizabeth McLean
Cover design by Steve Penner
Interior design by Margaret Ng
Typeset by Marjolein Visser
Photo credits: Daniel J. Cox/Natural Exposures iv, 6; Ed Kanze/ Dembinsky Photo Associates 18; Wayne Lynch 8, 10, 12, 16, 20, 22, 26; David Falconer/Folio 2; Mark Newman/Folio 4, 24; Walter Bibikon/Folio 14

Printed and bound in Canada

Library and Archives Canada Cataloguing in Publication
Swanson, Diane, 1944–
    Welcome to the world of kangaroos / Diane Swanson.
    Includes index.
    ISBN 1-55285-471-X
    1. Kangaroos—Juvenile literature. I. Title.
    QL737.M35S93 2004   j599.2'22   C2004-904187-8

For more information on this series and other Whitecap titles, visit our web site at www.whitecap.ca.

Thanks to David Morgan, University of Melbourne, Australia, and Derek Yalden, University of Manchester, United Kingdom, for their assistance.

The publisher acknowledges the support of the Canada Council for the Arts and the Cultural Services Branch of the Government of British Columbia for our publishing program. We acknowledge the financial support of the Government of Canada through the Book Industry Development Program for our publishing activities.

Contents

World of Difference

POGO STICKS WITH POCKETS.
That's what kangaroos are. They bounce up
and down on strong back legs while the
youngest—called joeys—ride in their mothers'
pouches. Having pocket babies makes
kangaroos "marsupials," mammals whose
young finish developing inside outer pouches.

There are more than 60 kinds of
kangaroos, and they range wildly in size.
The biggest, a red "roo," can be as tall as
a door and as heavy as a large man. At the
opposite end of the scale, a musky rat
kangaroo is just the size of a rat. Any kind
of kangaroo that weighs less than roughly

The largest
kangaroo in the
world is the big
red roo.

1

20 kilograms (45 pounds) is often called a wallaby.

Day and night, kangaroos see very well, and their large, well-placed eyes take in sweeping views. Their hearing is excellent, too. For the size of their bodies, most kangaroos have big ears. They can turn each one separately to pick up sounds from any direction. Even when the roos are

Huge eyes scan the wide world of the kangaroo.

feeding or resting, their ears are always swiveling.

The kangaroos' sense of smell is especially important when they're with other roos. Sniffing one another is a way of checking who's who and of finding a mate.

Many kinds of kangaroos live on their own for much of the time, but red and gray roos might feed in large groups, called mobs. Hundreds of eyes and ears alert to signs of danger make mealtimes safer for every kangaroo in the mob.

Kangaroos are amazing. Here's why:

- Searching for groundwater during dry times, some kangaroos dig pits more than a metre (3 feet) deep.
- Small kangaroos called potoroos can survive forest fires by hiding in underground burrows.
- Kangaroos on grasslands can hear rainstorms more than 30 kilometres (20 miles) away.
- Rat kangaroos use their tails to haul grass and leaves for nesting.

3

Where in the World

Kangaroos make themselves at home almost any place—even on a golf course.

KANGAROOS HAVE MANY NATURAL HOMES—in Australia and nearby islands, including New Guinea. But roos also live wild in New Zealand, where people once introduced them. Wallabies even moved into Great Britain and Hawaii—by accident. Years ago, they escaped from the people who brought them from Australia, made homes in the wild, and raised their young. Wallabies are still there today.

In Australia, kangaroos are found almost everywhere: in wet and dry regions, and in cold and hot temperatures. Some live on open grasslands and deserts, or in thick

5

forests. Other roos survive in the rockiest parts of the country.

For shelter, big kangaroos usually duck into dark caves or stand beneath leafy trees. Smaller ones creep into narrow ditches or crouch under bushes.

Only one kind of kangaroo lives underground. Rabbit-sized rat kangaroos called burrowing bettongs or boodies dig long

Some kangaroos, like this roo in New Guinea, live in trees.

networks of tunnels. Along these passageways, they often create more than 100 openings, which allow the animals to make quick exits and entrances. Several burrowing bettongs may share one set of tunnels.

You can guess where tree kangaroos spend much of their time—in trees. They climb onto branches, then curl up to rest or to sleep the day away. A Doria's tree kangaroo lives in New Guinea on mountain slopes as high as 4000 metres (13,000 feet)—the loftiest homes of any kangaroo.

KEEPING COOL

Kangaroos do what they can to avoid overheating. Many are most active at night—or in early morning and late afternoon—when it's cooler. They rest inside caves or plunk themselves down in the shade.

When kangaroos hop, they lose heat by sweating, then switch to heavy panting and drooling as soon as they stop moving. If they're still too hot, the roos lick their front legs. Heat from a mass of blood vessels escapes as the moisture dries, cooling the skin's surface.

World in Motion

BOING! BOING! BOING! The amazing jumping skills of kangaroos have made them world-famous. Some can easily cover more than 6 metres (20 feet) in a single bound. Gray roos can bounce 3 metres (10 feet) into the air, clearing a tall fence.

When kangaroos hop, they stand upright and use their springy back legs and feet. Long, strong tails sail through the air, pumping up and down and helping the roos keep their balance.

Big red kangaroos can cruise along at 32 kilometres (20 miles) an hour. In emergencies, they might double that speed,

Hippety-hop. An eastern gray kangaroo speeds across the plains.

9

On a hot day, a kangaroo prepares to take a cool dip.

but not for long distances. Surprisingly, it takes less energy for a kangaroo to travel fast—at least, at its cruising speed—than it does to hop more slowly.

When feeding, most kangaroos walk instead of hopping. They crouch over, planting all four feet on the ground, then move their legs ahead in pairs. Their tails act as fifth legs, supporting their body weight as the roos swing their back legs forward.

Some roos are great climbers. Stiff hairs around the back feet of rock wallabies help them travel easily across boulders. And the skid-free back feet of tree kangaroos work with long claws on their front feet to grasp branches and tree trunks. These kangaroos leap easily from tree to tree, as far as 9 metres (30 feet) at a time. They drop to the ground by sliding or stepping down backward.

Kangaroos can swim well, but they'd rather not—unless they're escaping heat, hunger, or danger, such as fire. Then they plunge into the water and paddle like dogs.

A mother kangaroo takes her joey into the water with her. By tightening her muscles, she closes the opening to her pouch, keeping a small roo safe while she swims. But a large joey might drown. The pouch usually can't close firmly around it or hold enough air for the roo to breathe.

11

World Full of Food

A hungry mob of kangaroos grazes the grass.

FROM GRASS TO MEAT IS WHAT KANGAROOS EAT. The food they prefer varies with their size. Small roos, such as rat kangaroos, eat fungi, plants, and some meat. Burrowing bettongs even nibble on dead sheep. Medium-sized roos, including swamp wallabies, depend on two types of food: grass and the tender leaves and stems of shrubs. Red kangaroos and other big roos are grazers. They can make meals of the toughest grass that grows in Australia's drylands.

All kangaroos use their front feet and hooked claws to help them eat. These

13

Near a bus stop, a quokka waits to beg treats from tourists.

handy paws can reach and hold food, and shove it into hungry mouths.

Most roos chew their food, swallow it, bring it back up, then chew it again lightly before reswallowing. For some, the process looks awkward and uncomfortable. They may suddenly pitch their heads back and heave violently to bring up the food, then ooze green liquid as they chew their meals for a second time.

Like other animals, kangaroos also need water. But many dryland roos get all they need from the dew on their food or the moisture inside roots, stems, and leaves. Unless plants dry up during weeks between rainfalls, these roos don't bother drinking from streams or ponds.

Where fresh water is scarce, tammar wallabies—which often live on islands—drink from the ocean. Their bodies are able to get rid of the extra salt.

Not all kangaroos stick to traditional foods. Some hang around parks where they find easy—and tasty—pickings from garbage cans and picnic tables. The roos develop a taste for human food, such as bread and sausages.

On Rottnest Island off west Australia, little kangaroos called quokkas or short-tailed wallabies seem to know when to expect tour buses. They wait for bits of bread that tourists toss to them. Although it's not recommended, some of the visitors even feed the quokkas by hand.

World of Words

KANGAROOS DON'T DO MUCH TALKING. They can't make many sounds. But if they're annoyed or frightened, some kinds of roos growl, hiss, or cough.

The burrowing bettong is one of the most talkative kangaroos—probably because it often lives with many other bettongs. As small as it is, it's usually loud, especially when squeaking and squealing.

Some playful joeys draw a CLICK, CLICK or a CLUCK, CLUCK from their mothers by vanishing from sight. Both red and gray roos call out loudly for

Western gray males issue threats by trying to appear extra large.

17

their babies. To reply, young joeys squeak, while older ones use their deepening voices.

Most kangaroos thump out signals by foot. As they start to hop away, they stomp down hard. Kangaroos all around respond to the alarm, bolting off even before they sense what the danger is.

Well-matched kangaroos may overlook threats and fight for a mate.

Sometimes roos thump to send messages to the animals that are hunting them. It's a way of saying, "Don't chase us. We know you're there."

Males competing for a mate may threaten each other. Some kinds rub their chests in dirt, yank up grass, or try to make themselves look bigger.

If threats are ignored, one male may challenge another by striking out with his front paws—often just hitting the air. Then the roos may box, but only if one is as big and as strong as the other.

WALLABY FIRE ALARM

In Australia's dry central region, called the Outback, a farmer discovered a wallaby that had been struck by a car. He took the animal home to care for it.

As the farmer slept that night, his house caught on fire. The wallaby did what frightened roos naturally do. It thumped out a warning with its strong back feet. The pounding woke up the farmer, who managed to get himself—and the wallaby—out of the house in time.

New World

JOEYS ARRIVE ALL YEAR ROUND—and at once, begin the most important journey of their lives. No bigger than beans, the hairless newborns must climb up to their mothers' pouches. They use only their front legs to crawl along tracks of fur, which their mothers lick to moisten.

Inside a pouch, a joey feels safe and warm. It can't see or hear, so it depends on its sense of smell to find a nipple. As it clamps down and starts to suck, the nipple swells, helping to hold the newborn in place. Now and then, the mother sticks her head into the pouch and licks the pocket clean.

Peek! A tammer wallaby takes a glimpse of its world.

For the first while, a joey does nothing but feed and sleep, sleep and feed. It grows very fast. In just six months, a red joey can grow to be 2000 times bigger than its newborn size!

Different kinds of joeys develop at different rates, but a red joey takes about four months to open its eyes. Soon after, the

Riding around in its mother's pouch is an easy way for a joey to travel.

little roo pokes its head out of its mother's pouch and takes its first peek at the world.

Another month or more might pass before the red joey ventures outside. But after a few minutes, it dives right back in, flipping a somersault to bring its head to the top of the pouch.

Each day, a joey spends a bit more time in the outside world. Its mother helps it get in and out of her pouch by loosening the muscles that control the size of the opening.

Kangaroos are usually born one at a time, moving into pouches all their own. But not always. The female musky rat kangaroo normally gives birth to twins, and now and then other kinds of roos also produce joeys in pairs.

The twins of one gray kangaroo grew too big to squeeze into her pouch at the same time. When one of them popped out for a while, the other tumbled in. The two joeys switched places so often that the mother grew tired and shooed both of them out.

23

Small World

A young kangaroo feeds by sticking its head into its mother's pouch.

LIFE AS A POCKET BABY ENDS ABRUPTLY. When a joey is three to ten months old—depending on the kind of kangaroo it is—a mother pushes it away. She has to free up her pouch before she gives birth again. But the young kangaroo, now no longer called a joey, stays close to her. It pokes its head inside her pouch to feed.

As months pass, the young roo learns what's best to eat by watching its mother. And it comes to know which animals to fear. Foxes, large lizards, and wild dogs called dingoes hunt kangaroos. Even eagles can be deadly, swooping down on small

25

roos and snatching them up with their sharp claws.

Roos usually hop away from their enemies, but big kinds sometimes try to fight back. Kangaroos might grab dingoes and drown them if the wild dogs chase the roos into streams or ponds.

A young kangaroo spends time learning to groom itself. Like adult

As a kangaroo grows, it learns all kinds of tricks—like balancing on its tail and scratching.

roos, it has a special comb for the job—the short second and third toes on each of its back feet. These toes are joined and work together to groom the fur on the animal's sides and around its ears.

Before roos are old enough to mate, they head off on their own. They keep growing, but as they age they grow more slowly.

Large kinds of kangaroos commonly live longer than small ones. A red roo, for instance, can reach age 15— about twice the age that a rat kangaroo might reach.

ROOS THAT ROMP!

Yanking mom's ear may not sound like a great game to you, but it's something that a young kangaroo seems to enjoy. In fact, it spends much of its time play-fighting its mother.

A little roo often starts a fight by hopping around wildly, kicking the air, then charging its mother. It may throw back its head, paw her shoulders and neck, and kick some more. The two of them "box" each other, imitating the fights that can break out between adult kangaroos.

27

Index